Hazel Bedazzled

Hazel
Lemon Squeezy

Written by
Tinka Ellington-Hooper

Illustrated by
Gladys Jose

To Emma,
Wishing you only sugar sweet moments in life.
Love, Tinka

Title: Hazel Lemon Squeezy
Author: Tinka Ellington-Hooper
Design: Gladys Jose

© Copyright 2015, Three Monkeys Publishing,
an Imprint of Educa Vision Inc., Coconut Creek, FL

Library of Congress Cataloging-in-Publication data available upon request.

All rights reserved. No part of this book may be reproduced or transmitted in any form or by any means, electronic or mechanical, including photocopying, recording or by information storage or retrieval system except by a reviewer who may quote brief passages in a review to be printed in a magazine or a newspaper without permission in writing from the author.

For more information, please contact:

Three Monkeys Publishing
2725 NW 19th Street,
Pompano Beach, FL 33069
www.ThreeMonkeys-Publishing.com

To Lily, Elena and Luisa,
the sweetest lemonade makers around.
With love,
Tinka

To my Grandma and my Mom,
"Todo obra para bien"
(Everything will work itself out)
I Love You,
Gladys

"This tree is making a mess of my yard," Hazel's dad complained while raking the leaves. "I'm going to cut it down," he grumbled, just as a lemon bonked him on the head.

"Nooo," Hazel shrieked, "Don't chop it down. Pleeeaase," she begged.

"Okay," he countered, "if YOU harvest the lemons, I won't cut it down."

"Deal!" Hazel agreed.

Hazel picked lemons all afternoon until her back was hurting and her basket was overflowing. "What am I supposed to do with all these lemons?" she asked herself when she was finally done.

"I could sell them. But who would want a basket full of lemons?" she wondered. "We could make silly looking lemon heads," she thought out loud. "But for that we need four, not forty."

"I've got it," she announced. "Let's set up a lemonade stand!" Her brother clapped his hands excitedly.

Hazel dragged the basket into the kitchen. She got out the big pitcher and filled it with water. She pulled out the sugar and a bowl of ice cubes. Lemonade tasted so much better cold.

Very carefully she cut each lemon in half and squeezed out the juice.

"This is going to take forever," she huffed as her eye fell on the blender.

Hazel had watched her mom use it many times, and it was always so fast. But her mom had told her not to touch the blender. It was too DANGEROUS.

She tiptoed to the kitchen window and peeked outside. Her dad was still working in the yard, and her mom had left for the store. "This is my chance," Hazel thought.

She stuffed the blender full of lemons and pushed the start button.

"Cool!" Hazel exclaimed, as she watched the lemons spin around. Suddenly the blender made a horrible grinding noise. Smoke was rising from the machine. It spun faster and faster.

"Uh oh," she winced as she tried to find the off switch. Right then the blender erupted like a volcano. Lemon chunks catapulted all over the kitchen. The sugar went flying. Her mom's favorite pitcher shattered onto the floor and water went EVERYWHERE.

"Oh nooooo," Hazel whined as she collapsed on the floor in the middle of the sticky, wet mess.

"What am I going to do now?" she cried. "When life hands you lemons, make lemonade," her grandmother always said when something didn't go as planned. By that she meant make the best of a bad situation and come up with Plan B. Hazel looked at the basket of lemons. It was still half full.

Then Hazel had an idea.

In Italy, people used to make grape juice by stomping on the grapes with their bare feet, Hazel remembered. She ran to the bathroom and filled the bathtub with lemons. She took off her socks and shoes and sniffed her feet.

"Good enough," Hazel decided, considering the slightly cheesy aroma coming from her toes.

She jumped into the tub. The juice was oozing through her toes and tickling her feet.

"Eeew," she screeched as she slowly put one foot down after the other. Soon she was stomping around and singing at the top of her lungs. Her dad poked his head in the door.

Her dad looked into the tub. "In that case shouldn't you close the drain?" "Oh nooooo," Hazel cried, as she realized her mistake. But by now the juice had already run out.

"What am I going to do now?" she cried. Only four lemons were left. "That's not enough to make lemonade."

"Don't be sad," her dad patted her on the back. "Tomorrow is Toby's birthday party and you will forget all about this. Plus, you know what grandmother always says."

"I know," Hazel grumbled,

"When life hands you lemons, make lemonade."

Suddenly she jumped out of the bathtub. "I've got it!" Hazel shouted. "Thanks Dad," she yelled, sprinting out of the bathroom. "You still need to clean up," her dad called after her, "and don't you touch that blender again."

Hazel's parents laughed when they saw what the noise was all about.

"So when life hands you lemons DON'T make lemonade?" her dad asked.
"Nope," Hazel grinned.

"Make Toby's favorite lemon cupcakes."

Comprehension Questions

Hazel Lemon Squeezy

What type of tree did Hazel's dad want to cut down?

What three ideas did Hazel have to make use of the lemons?

What would you do with a basket full of lemons?

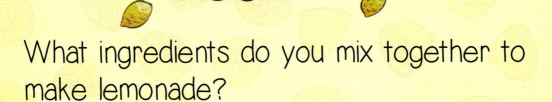

What ingredients do you mix together to make lemonade?

What did Hazel use in the kitchen that she wasn't allowed to?

Was it a good idea for Hazel to use the blender? Why or why not?

Hazel had several things go wrong. Did she give up or keep trying?

What does it mean when people say, "When life hands you lemons, make lemonade?"

What do you do when something goes wrong?

How do you solve a problem?

Hazel's Lemon Squeezy Cup Cake Recipe

INGREDIENTS

1 cup butter, softened
2 cups sugar
3 eggs
4 teaspoons grated lemon peel (2 lemons)
juice of 1 ½ to 2 lemons
1 teaspoon vanilla extract
3 ½ cups all-purpose flour
1 teaspoon baking soda
½ teaspoon baking powder
½ teaspoon salt
2 cups (16 ounces) sour cream

FROSTING

2 tablespoons of Greek vanilla yogurt
2 ¼ cups confectioners' sugar
2 tablespoons fresh lemon juice (or more if you like it more tart)

DIRECTIONS

The oven is going to be hot, so please be very careful and let a grown-up help you with the oven and with mixing.

1. In a large bowl, mix together all ingredients. Batter will be thick.

2. Fill greased or paper-lined muffin cups halfway with batter. Bake at 350° for 25-30 minutes or until a toothpick inserted near the center comes out clean. Cool for 10 minutes before removing from pans to wire racks.

3. For frosting, mix yogurt and confectioners' sugar in a small bowl until light and fluffy. Add the lemon juice, beat until smooth. Put frosting onto cupcakes.

Mmmmm, share with
friends and family and enjoy!

Tinka Ellington-Hooper was born and raised in northern Germany. In her search for white sand and warm sunshine, she found her true home in southern Florida, where she lives with her family and their big brown dog. When she isn't working on her books, she loves to spend time outdoors, going boating, biking or swimming with friends and family. She is a big believer in making lemonade out of not-so-sweet situations in life and really enjoys eating lemon cupcakes.

Gladys Jose was born and raised in Florida. As a young girl she would draw on anything she could get her hands on, sparking her love of art at an early age. Following that passion, Gladys graduated from the University of Central Florida with a B.F.A. in Graphic Design. By the time she graduated from college, she had developed her easy sense of humor, gift for illustration and her imagination to create entertaining and magical worlds for kids to enjoy.